World's Worst
FLOODS

Janey Levy

PowerKiDS
press

New York

Published in 2009 by The Rosen Publishing Group, Inc.
29 East 21st Street, New York, NY 10010

First Edition

Editor: Nicole Pristash
Book Design: Greg Tucker
Photo Researcher: Nicole Pristash

Photo Credits: Cover © Philip Wallick; p. 5 © Associated Press; p. 7 © Jim Wark/Peter Arnold, Inc.; pp. 9, 10–11 © Jim Reed/Getty Images; pp. 13, 17, 21 © Getty Images; p. 15 © Karen Su/Getty Images; p. 19 © Jim Holmes/Peter Arnold, Inc.

Library of Congress Cataloging-in-Publication Data

Levy, Janey.
  World's worst floods / Janey Levy. — 1st ed.
      p. cm. — (Deadly disasters)
  Includes index.
  ISBN 978-1-4042-4516-7 (lib. bdg.) ISBN 978-1-4042-4540-2 (pbk)
ISBN 978-1-4042-4558-7 (6-pack)
  1. Floods—Juvenile literature. I. Title.
  GB1399.L48 2009
  551.48'9—dc22
                                              2008010045

Manufactured in the United States of America

Contents

Destructive Water

A flood is the rising of a body of water over land that is generally dry. Some floods are small and do not cause much **damage**. However, some floods have washed away towns and have killed many people.

The deadliest flood in U.S. history happened in Pennsylvania in 1889. The South Fork Dam broke open and sent 20 **million** tons (18 million t) of water racing through the valley. The flood destroyed the town of Johnstown and killed more than 2,200 people. Other horrible floods have happened in many parts of the world. These floods have caused terrible **destruction**.

Here Johnstown villagers are shown near their homes after the Johnstown flood of 1889 destroyed much of their town.

Where Do Floods Happen?

Floods can happen anywhere there is a body of water. Rivers, lakes, and oceans can all flood land. River floods are common. In fact, most rivers **overflow** their banks about once every two years.

Floods happen around the world, from the United States, to Europe, to Asia. However, some places have terrible floods more often than others. China's history of flooding is the worst. In the midwestern part of the United States, the Mississippi River, Missouri River, and some smaller rivers flood often. In 1993, a flood in the Midwest caused about $15 million in damage and forced about 75,000 people from their homes.

This is Wakenda, Missouri, during the Great Flood of 1993. Almost all the homes in Wakenda were destroyed, and most of the townspeople moved away after the flood.

What Causes Floods?

Many things can cause a flood. The sudden melting of snow and ice produce river and lake floods. **Flash floods** are caused by too much rain in the mountains and in cities. Flash floods happen when heavy rain causes a lot of water to gather in a narrow space.

Lake floods happen when strong winds push water onto land. An **earthquake** can cause a lake flood by moving the water from side to side. Earthquakes can also produce giant waves in the ocean, called tsunamis, which cause flooding. Strong winds from **hurricanes** and other powerful storms can cause ocean floods, too.

This truck is driving through floodwaters caused by Hurricane Isabel in North Carolina.

Pages 10-11: Isabel's winds pushed ocean waves far onto land, flooding this town.

11

During and After a Flood

Floods are very dangerous. Floodwaters can easily drown people and animals. They damage and destroy cars, buildings, roads, bridges, and crops. Floods force people to leave their homes, and they can also **pollute** the water supply.

It may take days for floodwaters to **recede**. Then, buildings and belongings are covered with mud and destroyed. Water and food could be unsafe to drink and eat. There may not be power for lights, heat, or cooking as well. Flood damage like this is hard to fix. History has many examples of floods that have killed people and caused damage such as this.

Many days of heavy rain caused bad flooding in Meizhou, China, in 2007. The floodwaters damaged this house and left the ground covered with mud.

13

The Yellow River Floods

China has had many terrible floods. However, between November and July 1931, the Yellow River had the deadliest flood in history. The river overflowed, and water covered about 34,000 square miles (88,060 sq km). Between 1 and 4 million people died, and about 80 million people became homeless.

Up until 1931, the worst Yellow River flood happened in 1887. That year, a **dike** failed and sent floodwaters over the land. The water covered between 10,000 and 50,000 square miles (25,900–129,500 sq km). More than 1,500 towns and villages were flooded. Between 900,000 and 2.5 million people died.

China's Yellow River, shown here, has killed more people than any other river in the world. Because of this, some people call the river China's sorrow. "Sorrow" means "sadness."

The Johnstown Flood

In May 1889, heavy rain fell throughout western Pennsylvania. The rain filled lakes and rivers. A huge storm on May 30 brought even more rain. The South Fork **Reservoir** could not hold all the water, and its dam broke open on May 31. Twenty million tons (18 million t) of water spilled out of the dam.

A wall of water up to 100 feet (30 m) tall raced down the valley. The wall of water destroyed the town of Johnstown and several other villages. More than 2,200 people died, and the damage equaled more than $10 million. It was the deadliest flood ever in the United States.

This picture shows the pile of wood and steel that the Johnstown floodwaters carried through the town as the flood destroyed houses and other buildings.

17

Vietnam, in Asia, has suffered from terrible floods as well. In the 1900s, 26 big floods happened along Vietnam's Red River and Thai Binh River.

The Vietnamese build dikes along their rivers to try to stop floods from happening. In 1971, the dikes did not help. Heavy rains caused the dikes along the Red River to fail in several places. Floodwaters covered almost 618,000 **acres** (250,000 ha) of land. About 100,000 people died from the flood, and around 7 million tons (6 million t) of rice were destroyed. The flood had an effect on almost 3 million people altogether. It was Vietnam's worst flood of the century.

Here you can see homes flooded along the Red River in Hanoi, Vietnam. Parts of the city sit right on the banks of the Red River, and flooding happens often there.

Keeping Safe from Floods

Floods happen often around the world. Controlling them may be hard, but it is possible. Cities and towns use dams and dikes to keep water from reaching them. Some people build their houses high above the ground. Floods are a danger, but there are things you can do to stay safe.

If floods happen where you live, have supplies ready. Watch TV or listen to the radio if there is danger of a flood. Leave home if you are told to and go to higher ground. Do not try to drive or walk through floodwaters. These tips will help you stay safe from floods.

The long wall shown here is a levee. Levees are used to stop water from flooding land. If there is a flood, this levee will help keep people and houses safe.

21

Flood Facts

The Netherlands is a low, flat country in Europe. Dikes along the coast help keep out the sea. However, the dikes failed in 1530. The flooding killed about 400,000 people.

Huge storms caused terrible flooding in China in 1975. The Banqiao Dam and more than 60 other dams failed. Floodwaters covered more than 2 ½ million acres (1 million ha). Between 86,000 and 230,000 people died.

China's Yangtze River has more floods than the Yellow River does. A flood in 1931 covered more than 8 million acres (3 million ha) and killed 145,000 people.

The South American country of Venezuela suffered one of its worst floods in 1999. Almost 30,000 people died.

Glossary

acres (AY-kerz) Measures of land.

damage (DA-mij) Hurt done to buildings, roads, trees, and belongings.

destruction (dih-STRUK-shun) Great damage or ruin.

dike (DYK) A bank of earth built to control water.

earthquake (URTH-kwayk) A shaking of Earth caused by the movement of large pieces of land, called plates, that run into each other.

flash floods (FLASH FLUDZ) Floods that happen quickly.

hurricanes (HUR-ih-kaynz) Storms with strong winds and heavy rain.

million (MIL-yun) A very large number.

overflow (oh-ver-FLOH) To fill a space and spread beyond its borders.

pollute (puh-LOOT) To hurt with matter that is unsafe.

recede (rih-SEED) To back or move away from something.

reservoir (REH-zuh-vwor) A stored body of water.

Index

Web Sites

Due to the changing nature of Internet links, PowerKids Press has developed an online list of Web sites related to the subject of this book. This site is updated regularly. Please use this link to access the list:
www.powerkidslinks.com/disast/floods/

24